A CHRISTMAS SEQUENCE
AND
OTHER P̶

A CHRISTMAS SEQUENCE

AND OTHER POEMS

JOHN V. TAYLOR

THE AMATE PRESS

BRITISH LIBRARY CATALOGUING IN PUBLICATION DATA
TAYLOR, JOHN V.
A CHRISTMAS SEQUENCE AND OTHER POEMS
I. POETRY (RELIGIOUS)
I. TITLE
ISBN 0 947561 16 1

THE AMATE PRESS, 14A MAGDALEN ROAD, OXFORD OX4 1RW

PRINTED IN GREAT BRITAIN BY
PARCHMENT (OXFORD) LTD

AUTHOR'S NOTE

From time to time, especially in recent years, I have been moved to write something in verse to add to the Christmas card we send. There was always, however, a prior motive: the effort to compose has often been the only meditation and worship I have been able to make genuinely my own in the busy run-up to the Festival, the one sure means of recapturing for an instant a child's unique astonishment. Friends have occasionally asked whether I would publish these pieces, but I have judged the output too slight for that, until the generous urging of Anne and Vivian Ridler and Robin Waterfield encouraged me to place them in their hands.

Lullaby for the Unsleeping has already been published by Faber Music as a song with the music of Jonathan Harvey; and *Kestrels* was written for a collection of poems called 'Cathedrals', published in 1979 by the Winchester College Printing Society to celebrate the 900th anniversary of Winchester Cathedral; I gratefully acknowledge their permission to include them here.

While we were engaged to be married, my wife helped me to prune a lot of youthful verbiage from *Star*, and has remained my most perceptive encourager, so from the first the privacy of these poems has always been dedicated

TO PEGGY

with love

Contents

A Christmas Sequence:

  1. Annunciation   9

  2. Advent   10

  3. Angelus   11

  4. The Ass's Complaint   12

  5. Unicorn   13

  6. Christmas Venite   15

  7. Lullaby for the Unsleeping   16

  8. Madonna with Child dismembered   17

  9. One Cave   18

10. Under Snow   19

11. Presentation   20

12. Star   21

13. Dog in the Manger   22

14. Abba   23

15. To a Grandchild   24

16. Diptych   25

Lent   26

Easter   26

Kestrels returning to Winchester Cathedral   27

Circus   28

The Trap   29

Roots   30

Valentine   31

A CHRISTMAS SEQUENCE

1. Annunciation

Now she will always sit alone
on her high throne demure, becalmed
as a chit on the dunce's stool, or framed
in her own architectural space
who for our peace is now made icon,
captive child for goddess taken.

Yet fingertips cannot forget
textures of food, the spindle's weight
or furrowed grain of the scrubbed wood;
and eyes go searching for some other
wild girl whom the void calls mother
while the world turns within her womb.

2. Advent

Not yet the visitation in the night:
    children are marking time.
Not yet the promise of Messiah's might —
    O come, O come!

Not yet the birth. The crucible of her love,
    through the last month's frustrations
must nourish the unborn with essence of
    divine impatience.

The dream dies in plundered peasant eyes,
    and she will watch him grow
sick of the waiting game and set to seize
    the Not-yet now.

She it is will at last give him the cue,
    conspiring to arrange
that he, before his coming out is due,
    should take the plunge.

Now rumour of God's rule is in the air.
    He, knowing the Father near,
is rash enough to live as if it were
    already here.

Other such fools who follow from the first,
    though faithless and impure,
he welcomes, since forgiveness also must
    be premature.

He'll pay for it; and they will stop pretending.
    When make-believe has died,
then they will find the awaited Future standing
    at their side.

3. Angelus

But don't imagine you were the only
highly favoured one. There's no security
against this breaking and entering. We too
have felt the press, that excess
of presence cramming the breathless room
and, afterwards, the millstone of a new
life to be nurtured in secret.
The months mantled as prophets shuffled
past, scanning in sharper outline
the predicted flesh this God had taken
of concept, enterprise, or song.

All we lacked was your strength. Some chose
to terminate the obsession and make
out with mourning ghosts, while those
grown big with beauty crying to be told,
wrestled in sweat and groped to take
hold and thrust it into the light,
knowing before the end that what they
carried was a dead thing. Mother of God,
now and at the hour of his birth,
pray that we see alive between your hands
the poem we did not write.

4. The Ass's Complaint

As if it were not ache enough to have brought
the heavy-bellied girl day after day,
they leave me here untended to outstay
the blind sun bleaching the last stains of thought.

You, Manchild, wailing your first lungful there,
you might protest a grief worth braying for
had you to shoulder the rack-back load I bear,
or wait eternally at a whitewashed door.

5. Unicorn

They say it was her innocence drew him
down from the high places and the heath land.
Or was it the magnet of his intent
approach that brought her barefoot
to the meeting among the moonlit trees?

It was he, the chalky blur on the blackness
beyond the clearing, watching her
at ease on the sawn stump. Then the glance
of light off that long lance
tossed in salute as he dared and
crossed the impassable bright space.
Alien and fathomless his eyes
probed hers for mutual meaning,
till she saw the fine-drawn tear-drains
lining the pierrot mask and breathed
his acrid animal heat.
The brittle ivory of his limbs at last
folded to her feet and the sharp
imperious crest lay pressed
like a beam aslant her shoulder.
Sleeking the warm buckram of his ears,
she chanted as one in a dream:
> Stay, love, with me
> till we shall see
> all that is yet to be.

They came upon them there, the hunters,
in the dark time when the moon had set.
Because he was rare and mysterious
or because her embrace affronted them
or because they knew the going price
of the horn, but mostly because

it was a monstrosity, against nature,
to be one where always were two,
distinct and apart, they killed him.
Staunching the warm blood of his heart
she chanted as one in a dream:

> *Stay, love, with me*
> *till we shall see*
> *all that is yet to be.*

6. Christmas Venite

Let not my humble presence affront and stumble
your hardened hearts that have not known my ways
nor seen my tracks converge to this uniqueness.
Mine is the strength of the hills that endure and crumble,
bleeding slow fertile dust to the valley floor.
I am the fire in the leaf that crisps and falls
and rots into the roots of the rioting trees.
I am the mystery, rising, surfacing
out of the seas into these infant eyes
that offer openness only and the unfocusing
search for an answering gaze. O recognize,
I am the undefeated heart of weakness.
Kneel to adore, fall down to pour your praise:
you cannot lie so low as I have been always.

7. Lullaby for the Unsleeping

Close your eyes. You cannot out-stare the stars.
　　This is the hour when all good children are sleeping.
Is it the others you watch for, as though you knew
all that is done in the dark, as though you knew
　　this is not what I want to say to you?

Close your eyes' incomprehensible seas.
　　I cannot divine whether they shine with weeping
or brim with an ancient laughter. Do they show
imperious tides of joy, or do they show
　　oceans of unimaginable woe?

Close your eyes. For into their guileless gaze
　　the world will pour its pain, forever heaping
its anger on your heart, and you must bear
the outrage of its wounds and you must bear
　　the blame. Is it for this that you are here?

Close your eyes. The pale flame that plays
　　and pulses there is flaring out, is sweeping
across the empty dark and all of space
to embrace the galaxies, and all of space
　　spins back through these black holes and is your face.

Close your eyes? Erasing all that is?
　　Their ardent mirror carries in safekeeping
our dreamed existences. While my heart cries
for the folly of love's vigil, my heart cries:
　　'Though it last forever, never close your eyes.'

8. Madonna with Child dismembered

They have taken away my Lord, those puritans
of evidence and meaning. Yet not they
with all their chiselling doubt could so disface him.
My subtle Lord has taken himself away,
driven still by his will to be one of us,
the nameless multitude who have no faces,
dare to bestow no presence each to other,
nor can meet love when it directly gazes,
trusting only its merest casual traces.
As when the sun, long down, fires the cold skies,
kindling the feathery drifts of upper air,
so, Mother, your deep ecstasy embraces
my godlessness. All Bethlehem's in your eyes
and in your peace I know your son is here.

9. One Cave

One cave is very like
another. Rumour too late
smouldering over the hill
summoned me breathless down
the sheeptracks. Around the well
shrill twittering children reiterate
this as the place.

                              Fresh
donkey's dung at the door the only
evidence of arrival and departure.
This bare stage of staled straw
has seen no play, other
than birth and passing of beasts.
Yet I stand scenting the trace
of my own kind lingering
like smutch of candles quenched.
Nothing remains to hold
me here but the hollow plainly impressed
in the hay trough. Still the starling voices
chime faintly. I stoop, fingering
the firm fineweave bowl of the nest
that is the measure and mould
of my untenanted heart.

10. Under Snow

The gentle legends fall like festive snow
muffling in drifts of miracle the event.
Dig for the sharp-edged fact obscured below
the wintry straw, the lullaby lament
of gothic northlands. Was old Helena's cavern
any less fanciful? Soon as the telling began
the child was swaddled in portents fondly woven
to show a birth that matched the full-grown man.

Ah, here's the rock beneath the fantasy:
there was a man, surpassingly alive
whose own truth blazed with such authority
as made the simple and the poor derive
all faith from his and, seeing the road he trod.
they had no heart for any other god.

11. Presentation

Pangs to bring forth the meaning are severer
    than labour on the straw.
What manner of God was sovereign heretofore,
    that a birth should bring him nearer?

Pondering still, adrift in a dream, she stands
    upon the marbled splendour
and must for the first impossible time surrender
    her son to strangers' hands.

Her gaze falls to a flagstone, raised and riven
    by one pale seedling's power
and, blindly blundering close upon the flower
    a bullock, doomed and driven.

Her guardian fingers, swooping into pain,
    are trampled and defiled;
she hugs them to herself and finds her child
    is in her arms again.

Noondark the temple reels. She understands
    no Lord sits on the throne
but this omnipotence that split the stone
    and stretched and tore her hands.

12. Star

Love knows the anguish of their sullen cry
    who seek so long
        in vain
the time-locked secret of the emblazoned sky.
Love sends a star into the menacing gloom,
    welcomed with song
        and pain,
hanging in loneliness to bring them home.

13. Dog in the Manger

Come to think of it there must have been
a dog in the manger cocking a culprit eye —
'Only warming the hay' — cuffed off the scene.
He never was one for letting sleepers lie.

Twelfth Night came. It laughed to see such sport,
baying the star and nipping the camels' heels,
exciseman's nose probing the smells they brought,
crookleg thumping fleas as the company kneels.

Now with outrageous confidence it may take
its place at all our high solemnities.
Carpaccio, Corregio, van Eyck
let the dog in, knowing what pain it is

to run the streets in renegade repute,
faithful even to death and yet unclean,
since none forgets the muzzle of the brute
lapped beggars' sores and blood of a tumbled queen,

and still betrays the dustbin runabout.
Whatever longing urged it to the stable,
its infidel fidelity does not doubt
that crumbs fall freely from this master's table.

14. Abba

All the small children called their fathers *abba*,
Daddy come. Why, Daddy? Daddy kiss.
But he alone blasphemed prattling to heaven
the Word's first word
here in the sawdust, there before time was.
Always it was *abba* save for the sole cry
Eloi! why? —
even then murmuring into the absent hands
not formless sigh of being,
infinitely breathed OM,
but soft plosive breaking of the waters,
birth into body and blood,
far-off mallet thud and three days' pause
before release of life,
expiration of spirit into our hearts
crying *abba*, Father.

15. To a Grandchild

Over the swinging parapet of my arm
your sentinel eyes lean gazing. Hugely alert
in the pale unfinished clay of your infant face,
they drink light from this candle on the tree.
Drinking, not pondering, each bright thing you see,
you make it yours without analysis
and, stopping down the aperture of thought
to a fine pinhole, you are filled with flame.

Give me for Christmas, then, your kind of seeing,
not studying candles — angel, manger, star —
but staring as at a portrait, God's I guess,
that shocks and holds the eye, till all my being,
gathered, intent and still, as now you are,
breathes out its wonder in a wordless yes.

16. Diptych

He who lay curled in Mary's womb,
starting and ending in a cave,
has broken new-born from the tomb.

His star outshone the smothering gloom,
searching for those he came to save.
He who lay curled in Mary's womb.

to take upon himself our doom,
and our unkindnesses forgave,
has broken new-born from the tomb.

Again they offered sweet perfume,
myrrh for his helpless limbs they gave,
he who lay curled in Mary's womb.

Swaddling allows too little room;
he that was bound from crib to grave
has broken new-born from the tomb.

Angels again brought tidings: 'Whom
seekest thou? See, the Lord you crave,
he who lay curled in Mary's womb,
has broken new-born from the grave.'

Lent

Jogging blind through winter's leaflessness
we must last out this marathon of cold,
though grime gathers under the grey duress
and faith is grown old.

Give back our springtime so the first petals' pink
falls like alleluias through the melting air,
deep in the loose loam let the gnarled roots drink
and clenched ferns open to the sun in prayer.

Easter

At a turn of the head bent intent on a task,
ripple of light, hem of his garment only,
or lift of the heart suddenly less lonely
is all the Easter evidence I ask.

Kestrels returning to Winchester Cathedral

Look, the kestrels are back on the tower's crest,
not nesting yet but breasting the wafture of air
up the grey cliff, questing remembered bounds
of their green kingdom, sending tenuous
couriers of fear to mark their tribute down.
They ride, glide; a flicker of feathered fire
lifts them higher and still, so still, they mount, they aspire.

Their rock face beckons beneath the changing skies,
milky under the moonrise, scintillant at noontime:
Who shall ascend into the hill of the Lord?
'Climb!' says the stone, 'but first feel with your eyes
the massive weight, the rough male surfaces
hatched and rimpled for joy of the solid fact.
Touch and believe, lay hand to my scars, and climb.'

They who are caught in the lure of the vision of God
endure the lost vision. As they plod
upward, the ridges veil the pure pale summit.
Now the rhythm is all. They hoist and haul
their own dead weight on pinnacles and gullies,
scale the wet shale, cling to the wind-whipped wall
till the iron of the rock be formed in the unsure flesh.

Only then shall the sesame door of grace
show the more excellent way. Enter alone
and see where all was mass now all is space;
no more a mountain, this, but fountains of stone
or files of lifted wings, trecento descants
sprung from a long-sustained gregorian tone.
Let the heart soar through falling flakes of fire,
hover higher and still, so still, mount and aspire.

Circus

Pitiful blinded ape
to let them drape that rippling
drum of muscle and hair,
sporting a surplice down
to your soft shuffle, and all, poor clown,
to make the round O gape.

The grubby cotton above
your dexterous glove beating
time barely conceals
that rosary loop of chain;
your impudent lips invite again
the laughter that you crave.

You hoot your hideous hymn
and, as the acclaim explodes,
hammer your iron bowl
in frantic self-applause.
Then the split coconut jaws
yawn wide and scream, and scream.

Silence sudden as frost
falls across the ring.
The crumpled dish drops
like a discarded prayer.
One polished paw scrawls on the air,
God help us, the sign of the cross.

The Trap

That long wire letterbox lying
in wait like a bad pun among
the lettuce, is a cage we set in
shamefaced rage to get the squirrels,
agile assassins of fragile unfledged
birds. But traps are indiscriminate.
It was a hedgehog we found wedged
at the end of the narrow box at the end
of the long day, its taut spines
caught in the mesh, penned by the
bristling urge to defend that midmost
flesh. There it had curled, had cringed,
a dusty peasant at prayer, a child
unborn though it reeked already of death.

After my fingerprick fumbling my wife
twirled its world over so the hinged
flap fell flat and left it within light
of the house with a yard-off baitful of milk.
We never saw it come to life,
but in the twinkling of a mere minute
we leaned out breathless at the sight:
as one brindled beast guzzled,
a pygmy replica clowning around
like a toy on wheels nuzzled her side.

Is it the abrupt upside-downing
that does the trick, or the warm archaic
scent of the solacing milk that smoothly
wipes from the air the stale decaying
taint that was not death but fear,
and sleeks the entangled needles free?
Seeing them glide erratically under
the hem of the dark and disappear,
I wonder that, for all my praying,
no one has done the same for me.

(29)

Roots

I knew the house had gone but did not think
that lawn and lane and orchard would explode
into this ash-grey land, fields be upthrown
to raise this giant barrow of the motorway,
the shaded pond, where cattle swung to drink,
laid out and lidded below this monstrous slab
inscribed line upon line with pallid homes
cowering under the mindless roar of the road.

No ghost. No relic. Only the locked church
to give a bearing. Other men's walls forbid
my pilgrim pieties. Call off the search
for fragrant images none will recompose —
the embracing hearth where spent logs collapsed
to a feathery bed, the aromatic passage
through the padded door, the high bay where the sun
caressed his desk and always one red rose.

I breach the embankment by the underpass.
Between the obscenities and the football teams
I conjure poppies splashed on the orchard grass;
the vanished pear tree draws me. Through long dreams
its snow has glimmered, its amber-beaded arms
have lifted me to the clouds when none could guess
the bite of the axe, the tearing fall, the smirch
of that white glory, nor this wilderness.

Clear of the tunnel I turn and see it stand,
a tender ten-year stripling of wild pear,
the opening buds not white but stippled crimson.
So. It has lived in the dark, lived to endure
its unremitting hurt of amputation,
stretching blind subterranean branches lower
to bind together rocks and clay and sand,
and from the pain this tree, this new bright flower.

(30)

Valentine

To say I love you is like saying 'God'.
In Eden once I knew what both terms meant;
each was distinct, known or becoming known,
until, beyond the Image, I faced the Other
and knew not how to love that counter-self
in you or him, which might reject, or smother;
and above all I feared my nakedness.
Yet still my heart is yours, yes, more than his,
and his, 'Where art thou?' echoes only mine
calling for you among the tangled trees.

'God' is my dread, my hunger and my hope
thrown on the luminous screen of the outer dark
while, hidden at the inmost core of me,
he who is not I waits my coming home.
You too, dear love, draw me to that labyrinth:
while needing most your separate otherness,
I cannot reach you till I find my self.
The more I pick these ravelled threads apart
the more they fray. Forgive me, patient heart,
that I bring nought today but a lover's knot.